Glimpses of a
Forever Foreigner

Poetry & Artwork

Inspired by Japanese American

Experiences

Poems *by* **Lawrence Matsuda**

Artwork *by* **Roger Shimomura**

Printed by CreateSpace *An Amazon.com Company*
Charleston, SC • www.CreateSpace.com

Library of Congress Catalog Number: 2014910912

Introduction

During World War II, 120,000 Japanese and Japanese Americans from four far western states and Alaska were incarcerated in ten American concentration camps, some for more than three years. They were charged with no crime. The cause of their imprisonment was their ancestry. The Minidoka War Relocation Center was one such concentration camp. Three individuals, Gordon K. Hirabayashi, Fred T. Korematsu, and Minoru Yasui, challenged various aspects of the exclusion order and mass detentions through the judicial system. All three cases were heard by the US Supreme Court, which ultimately upheld the legality of the government's actions. In a fourth case, Mitsuye Endo, who had gone to a camp with her family, sued the United States for her release from within it. Paradoxically, on the same day that it convicted Korematsu, the Supreme Court ordered her release saying that, "As a loyal American, she should be free to come and go as she pleases."

Anxious to prove their loyalty, many Nisei, or second-generation men volunteered from camps, as well as from other parts of the United States and Hawaii, to fight in Europe and the Pacific. Most served in the segregated 442nd Regimental Combat Team/100th Battalion which fought in Italy and France and suffered high casualties. The 442nd/100th became one of the most decorated units in American history. Nisei also served in the Military Intelligence Service (MIS) as translators in the Pacific. Other Japanese Americans showed their resolve by refusing to be drafted as long as their families were kept in a concentration camp. Most who did were tried for their actions, convicted, and sent to federal prisons.

After the war, the lingering effects of discrimination remained as the Japanese and Japanese Americans attempted to rebuild their lives.

One former Minidoka resident said, "When World War II started, they forced us to leave home and I didn't want to go. When the war ended they kicked us out of camp even though we had nowhere to go." Over the years, the negative Japanese stereotypes persisted in discriminatory laws that prevented intermarriage, land ownership, and the ability to become naturalized citizens. In addition, the media continued its stereotypic depictions of Japanese and Japanese Americans as sly, sneaky, and untrustworthy. With the outbreak of the Korean War, the Japanese stereotype was transferred to the Red Chinese enemy and then to the Viet Cong during the Vietnam War. For all intents and purposes, the World War II Japanese enemy was reincarnated and served as a Hollywood Asian stereotypic staple in the 1950s through the 1980s.

After a long movement for redress, eventually supported by the vast majority of Japanese Americans, Congress passed the Civil Rights Act of 1988, which awarded a one-time, tax-free payment of $20,000 to each Japanese American who had been in a camp and was still alive on the day that the bill became law. President Reagan signed the bill, along with a letter of apology, which cited the causes of the injustice: *race prejudice, war hysteria, and a failure of political leadership.*

Even though a formal apology was given, there still remains the possibility that the injustice will happen again to other racial groups especially when fear and frenzy rule. As a result, it is the legacy of the Japanese American experience to serve as a reminder to never let it happen again.

Lawrence Matsuda, PhD, with scholarly assistance from Dr. Roger Daniels, Charles Phelps Taft Professor Emeritus of History, University of Cincinnati.

Background

In 1942, Roger Shimomura was a youngster at the Minidoka War Relocation Center along with his family. In 1945, Lawrence Matsuda (number 11464D) was born there. At that time, Matsuda's relatives were either in American concentration camps or at the family home in Hiroshima, Japan. For both Roger and Lawrence, the forced incarceration experience and continuing after effects were major influences in their art. Recently both presented at the Minidoka Pilgrimage Reunions and Civil Rights Symposiums in Twin Falls, Idaho, regarding the effects of the injustice.

Glimpses of a Forever Foreigner grew out of their common interest in the incarceration and their desire to express their concern about the injustice. Roger read Lawrence's unpublished poetry manuscript and selected twenty-one poems to illustrate. Eighteen illustrations were created specifically for the book. The cover and three others were from his existing work.

The poems are arranged in chronological order except for *Barry the Psychiatrist*, which begins the collection. Thereafter, the topics move from the 1942 forced incarceration to the period after the war, then to friends/family, and end with the Fukushima disaster.

Acknowledgments

Faceless appears in the Black Lawrence Press 2011 National Poetry Month website, http://blacklawrence.wordpress.com/2011/04/29/national-poetry-month-spotlight.

No No Darkness, *Barry the Psychiatrist*, and *They Turn Their Eyes Away* appear in *The Seattle Journal for Social Justice*, Volume 11, Issue 1, Summer 2012. Seattle University School of Law.

Hiroshima Bomb appears in *Plumepoetry.com*, Issue 21, 2013.

Saturday Matinee I ~ The Spy, Saturday Matinee II ~ Pacific Hell, and *Saturday Matinee III ~ Mickey Rooney Does Yellow Face* appear in *Malpais Review*, Volume 3, #3, Winter 2012-2013.

1943 Minidoka, Idaho Concentration Camp Veil and *1943 Minidoka Camp Album* — will appear in *Zero Ducats* in 2014.

Salmon Dreams I ~ The Priest, Salmon Dreams II ~ The Haunting, and Salmon Dreams III ~ Salmon Rise, and *Wisp of a Girl* appear in *Plumepoetry.com*, Issue 22, 2013.

Tsunami Letter appears in *Plumepoetry.com*, 2014.

WWII Route to Freedom appears in *Raven Chronicles*, Volume 19, Winter 2012-13.

La Medusa Cooking Class appears in the Reviews Section of La Medusa Restaurant website, 2009, www.lamedusarestaurant.com.

Woman Who Paints with Fire appears in the Black Lawrence Press 2012 National Poetry Month website, http://blacklawrence.wordpress.com/2012/04/06/national-poetry-month-spotlight.

Nazi Death Train appears in the Black Lawrence Press 2014 National Poetry Month website, http://www.blacklawrence.com/national-poetry-month-spotlight-lawrence-matsuda-2.

Careening Toward Forever After appears in *Plumepoetry.com*, Issue 34, 2014.

Table of Contents

Part V: Friends & Family

Part VI: The Way Infinity Turns

Appendix

Artwork Titles

Part I:
Japanese American Concentration Camp

During World War II, 120,000 Japanese and Japanese Americans were incarcerated in ten American concentration camps for approximately three years. They did not commit a crime or receive due process. Minidoka was one such camp. To prove their loyalty, some young Nisei men volunteered to fight for the US in Italy. Based on the success of the all-Japanese 442nd Regimental Combat Team, a mandatory military draft was implemented in the camps.

Barry the Psychiatrist

Without a greeting at Thanksgiving,
Barry approaches me and insists that
my mother was under
great stress before my Minidoka* birth.

He believes my DNA stress switches
were turned off in the womb
and anxiety tolerance levels raised.

As a child Barry survived
a Jewish resettlement camp
in Poland after the war.
He says both of us *need* chaos —
our bodies can withstand hunger
longer than most. Good times
and happiness make us nervous,
we compensate by overeating, risking diabetes.

He claims my mother never gave
me the "facial shine" of love as a baby,
a look both he and I crave as adults.

Good day Barry,
my response to his early afternoon
discourse without preparatory niceties.

*Mother always had a shine
for her grandson, Matthew,* I reply,
being glad for my son.

Barry wrinkles his forehead. *I know,* he says,
and then resumes his "prenatal stress effects" diatribe.

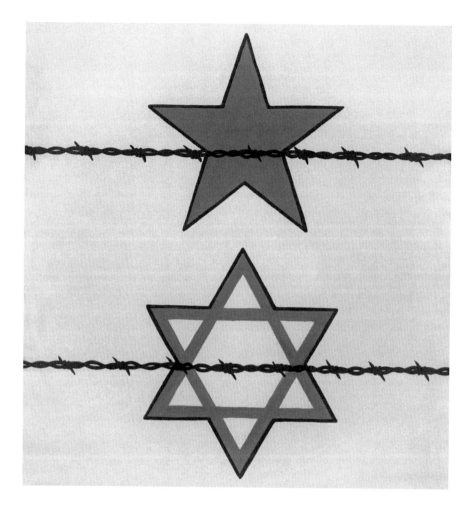

Mentally I curl up in a ball,
mainline internal chemicals again.
All those prenatal stresses pump fresh in my veins.
Like a heroin addict I don't want them
to degrade over time like radiation
and leave no trace of why I want to chew nails,
burn ladders, and stomp the sake cup.

Minidoka was a Japanese American WWII concentration camp in Idaho.

1943 Minidoka Camp Album

Cradled in a grim carpenter's lap,
a coal-eyed infant
glows in the camp photograph.

Years later I learn
the elderly couple
prayed for a child, cherished the baby,
helplessly watched its last breath
before this photo was taken.

> *Is it a real infant's face*
> *or a black-and-white*
> *shadow cast between*
> *a carpenter's suspenders?*

Button is an eye,
open-collar curve
resembles a head.

Temperatures drop, distortion bends
a mirror reflection,
my mind falls like Alice
down a rabbit hole.
I push tingling fingers
through a mist, touch something cool.

Dead carpenter and child
no longer exist as slick
paper shadows.

In my closeness I know them.
Their names, anxious to be heard,
sizzle like glowing embers
on my tongue.

1943 Minidoka, Idaho
Concentration Camp Veil

Auntie Shizuko communicates with voices beyond the veil:

It is our destiny to be in hell,
purgatory where our
spirits will be pulled
slowly from our
souls through silver cords
that wrap our bodies
around a cross.

Feet will be the first
to feel flames. Odors like
the stench of 10,000 cattle
snorting in cages fume.
Their necks held tight between
bars snare muzzles in feed. Half-blind
in narrow passageways,
they march heavily down chutes,
too trusting to suspect
the bloody hammer.

Glistening steel latrine troughs
run red, yellow, and brown in camp.
Water cascades like surf breaking,
stench flushes past all.

Private functions on display,
Mother's modesty battered.
She covers her head
with a paper bag to guard
what dignity remains.

Nocturnal habits emerge —
prehistoric survival patterns burn
cycle shifts, internal clock
sets midnight relief sessions —
obsessive habit like a facial tick carted
back to Seattle, remnant of a time
when bathroom doors
were luxuries.

Camp Wings

Dust, *bachan's** daily guest,
collects on shelves, corners
and settles on cracked window sills.

She believes *Kamisan*,
god of nature,
sends twisting sand devils,
spirits to rouse her from bed
for mindless routines:
hike half a mile to the gang latrine,
wipe greasy grit from mess hall metal trays;
consume wieners, Vienna sausage,
and organ meats ground
beyond recognition, food her body
barely accepts.

*Jichan** gathers wood scraps,
scavenges nails from wooden boxes,
carefully pounds the bent ones
straight on a concrete slab,
cobbles a bird house.
Sparrows live here,
black-and-white
messengers remind *bachan*
of life beyond endless boredom
and fears of becoming a desert.

Like Noah's doves,
sparrows dive and scour
miles of desert,
search for an olive branch,
twig that would deliver *bachan* home.

---

*Bachan is grandmother and Jichan is grandfather.

Idaho does not accept our dead.
Twin Falls mortuaries
reject Minidoka Japanese.

Dr. Abbot calls Aunt Amy's time.
Medics in whites gently slide
her from the bunk
for a journey to Salt Lake City,
first excursion outside prison gates.

Cousin Hisako snatches
shadows passing in her dreams.
Don't worry, Amy whispers,
tell Tetsuo I am fine.

Tetsuo, her son, a US soldier,
volunteers from Minidoka
to defend freedom in Europe.
He takes aim and blasts a padlock,
gates of Dachau swing open.

Nazis have no coal,
crematoriums silent,
odors of death permeate the air,
something like a mixture
of chocolate pudding, urine,
feces, and rotting meat.
Naked bodies stacked
like tangled tree limbs,
pungent fluids trickle down drains.

In Minidoka coal rages in potbelly stoves.
When did we hear of crematoriums?
It seems we knew.
It seems we always knew.
When our boys came home
we knew for sure.

They Turn Their Eyes Away

Minidoka barbed wire
snags hope like tumbleweed.
One thousand miles away
at Tule Lake, California,*
Shoichi Okamoto twists and falls,
a bullet in his head,
cost of disbelieving a guard.
The soldier walks free,
fined a dollar for "unauthorized use
of government property."

Wind blows alkaline dust
through the tarpaper barrack.
Bachan prays for freedom,
strikes her singing bowl.

Minidoka crumbles in her dreams
when black rain splatters Hiroshima
and sunlight sparkles silver
through thin barrack doors.

Freedom will not be open arms
and Welcome banners.
Red rose petal showers
reserved for *real* Americans.
We are the vanquished foe
walking through the victor's lair,
gauntlet of 1,000 eyes.
Anxious to pass unnoticed
in our yellow skin,
we will turn away from
Remember Pearl Harbor remarks.
Mushroom clouds inhabit
the irises of our eyes.

---

*Site of a Japanese American concentration camp during World War II.

Part II:
World War II & Beyond

"History does not repeat itself, but it rhymes."

~ Mark Twain

No-No Darkness

Suto-san refuses machine guns
and foxholes in Italy,
checks "No-No"
on the US loyalty questionnaire,
avoids the camp military draft.

Minidoka bunk, young wife
and two baby girls traded
for steel bars and hard time
at McNeil Island Federal Pen.

His "No-No" brand exiles
him to purgatory littered with
conscientious objector leper rags,
an untouchable pariah.

Upon his release, old friends
cross the street to avoid him.
Others refuse to shake his hand.

He acts and looks like a regular Joe
after President Truman's pardon.
Gossip pursues him until he dies,
no forgiveness from Japanese neighbors.

He never asks for pardon,
lives his life in joy and celebration,
concocts his secret *tsukenomo* recipe,
pickled cabbage full of zest and magic
fermented under a large stone for weeks,
Japanese sauerkraut fumes noxious fragrances
when the lid is popped.

He always shares a jar with me.
In its salty tang,
I can taste the "No-No"
depth of his resolve.

Hiroshima Bomb *for Annie's mother*

Confetti spirals flutter into dark green.
Cousin Mary and her *bachan**
stand on the Hiroshima pier.
Horns blare as the last steamship
pulls away before the war,
separating her from Mom and Dad.

In her black and white
grammar school girl uniform,
Mary looks Japanese.
American gait draws
every neighbor's stare,
gaijin, foreigner.

Return to Sender letters
from America.
Bachan seeks a temple psychic:

*Mary's parents are well in a hot
and desolate place.
Razor points at intervals
confine thousands.*

*A gourd of death
will tumble from blue
Hiroshima skies.*

*No chance to scream,
glass shards explode,
flesh burns,
no chance to breathe.*

*Victorious Americans will
toss chocolate to orphans.
Your outstretched palm
will catch nothing.*

Mary rides the Tokyo express
through Hiroshima after the bomb.
Blinds pulled tight, sunlight
seeps through cracks.

Twenty US Army soldiers
rise silently,
their khaki garrison
caps cover hearts,
they kneel, fill the aisle,
heads bowed as if in church.

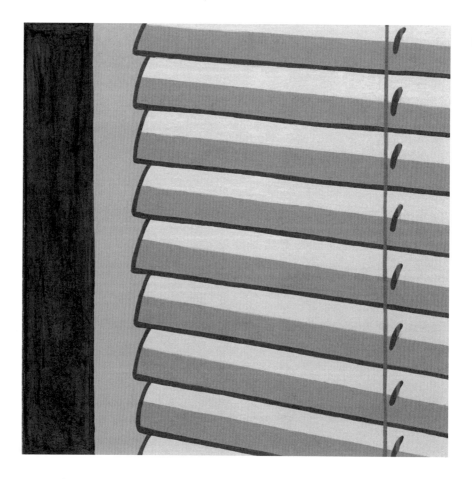

Mary slides to the window,
raises the curtain
to a bleached moonscape
of stacked and mangled heaps.

School boy in gray underwear
pulls a red wagon against the wind.
His fluttering oilskin umbrella
whips inside out, tearing parchment from spines
in the feted horizontal rain.

---

* Grandmother in Japanese.

Gates of Dachau

for T/4 Ichiro Imamura & the 552nd Artillery Battalion

Walking skeletons
of gray flesh rise
from mounds scattered
over a frozen field.

Hollow eyes and stench
repulse Ichiro, as he waves
Hershey bars and Spam.

Japanese American soldiers fear typhus
when prisoners fall to their knees.
Survivors grasp US khaki coat tails,
kiss combat boots, sniff clean trousers, and smile
through scurvy-ridden gums,
speak languages garbled
and confused like their bodies.

Sagging black-and-white striped rags
suspended by bones,
dance a circle around a dead horse
on the side of the road.

Prisoners devour strips of carrion.
Some die gorging more than
their bodies can tolerate.

Chalky oval bars,
engraved with numbers,
stacked in neat lines,
souvenirs Ichiro desires to liberate.
He gives no thought to the bars' contents,
thanks God his family and relatives
are alive and safe
in American concentration camps.

WWII Trophies

A US Army kill team stationed in Afghanistan was convicted of collecting body part souvenirs in 2011.

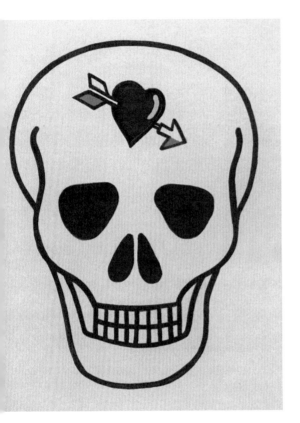

Lines of Japanese ears dangle from a few American ammo belts during the war, gold teeth melt into bullion.

"Coconuts" thud on the deck of PT 209. Top Kick hollers, *This batch is ripe, boys. No gold or ears here.*

A basket drops overboard, submerges into green waters. Faces disappear in salt.

Life magazine runs a photo —
Arizona woman sends a *thank you* to her
boyfriend for the autographed skull.
Roosevelt receives a bone;
disgusted, he orders it buried.

Twenty years later
Japanese bones return.
Auntie Miyo opens the box,
peers deeply into
the half-empty container.

She props a photo in the family shrine,
places rice in the gold chalice,
and chants a Buddhist prayer.

Ushina wareta-monowa, ni-doto modoranai
That which is lost, will never return.

In my unconsciousness nothing dissolves.
Before the interval when sleep grips,
images of lost things flash
like stampeding ghost horses anxious to return.

They churn the ground until a crevice opens.
I toss the pain of my father, my mother, of all
those who suffer real and spiritual disintegration
in war and in the daily banishments of their differences.

Luckily they come back to me so I can speak to them
and tenderly hold them as they could not be
held while they lived.

Nazi Death Train

Under a French full moon,
the Bordeaux Express flies
a crooked German flag.
Wheels screech and spark.
Helmeted Nazi guards leap,
gravel flies as jackboots skid,
wool overcoats flutter like capes in the night.
Mauser carbines held at the ready.
Cattle car chains rattle,
human cargo falls silent.

Overlooking the tracks,
six-year-old Arlette shivers, holds
her breath, stretches her hat over eyes.
She and grandfather
nest in tall grass.

Like an electric shock, a white flash
on the hill catches a Nazi eye.
Arlette's grandfather rolls her over,
blots her underwear from sight.

Flashlight beams pierce blackness
seeking the patch of white,
pointed guns locked and loaded.

The guard's thoughts drift:

> *Comforting summer grass,*
> *bed where he and his lover curl.*
> *Her underwear gleams like a beacon to outer space.*
> *Soft lips press and silk stockings beg to be free.*

He dreams of warm stone hearths,
dinner tables set in expectation, welcoming arms,
lovers embracing. In this world,
all soldiers come home safely even
in the darkest night.

Arlette's goose bumps rage,
train piston rods muscle
iron wheels with a chug
and steam blast.
Guards snag handrails,
swing and leap
like trapeze flyers
onto metal platforms.

Clouds smother the moon,
sanctuary beckons,
tomorrows will be better
than yesterdays for Arlette.

Worker bees will flee to honey domes at dusk
and starlings will squabble in fig trees
when Arlette opens a trunk,
presses her mother's
white lace wedding dress
to her cheek.

Part III:
The Silver Screen

*In Hollywood, the inscrutable Japanese enemy stereotype of
World War II lasted for years as it evolved into North Koreans, Viet Cong,
and Chinese Communists on the silver screen.*

Bandages unwind
from the World War II
white lieutenant's visage —
the surgeon reminds him
that a Japanese face will be
his forever.

The soldier nods heroically,
cost of being an Anglo-American
spy in Japan.

The organ music rises
and trumpets blare
for the reveal.

A monster fills the mirror —
six foot tall, doughy nose, slant eyes.
He speaks *baka** Japanese,
stresses the wrong syllables
with a thick American accent
fooling only himself.

Surely the surgeons recognize their Frankenstein,
but all are convinced: spy-shaped
eyes will magnetize secrets.
In real life this charade would
end in torture and a firing squad.

I wonder, as a teenager,
if surgery would let me pass as white?
I would eat tuna casserole,
Swiss steak with ketchup,
plus macaroni and cheese
to complete my disguise.

Years later at a Halloween celebration
in Seattle's Columbia City,
a white man dresses as a coolie:
Fu Manchu mustache, long braided que,
spectacles, shiny silk cap, eyeliner, and black
high-necked pajama jacket with gold brocade.

I shoot him the "hate" stare,
piercing glare I experienced myself.
With a sneer I disdainfully examine him
with X-ray vision from top to bottom
as if he were a single cell specimen
floating in a petri dish.
He squirms, fidgets, knots into a ball
and shrinks from sight.
I have no costume, no makeup,
my eyes, like the rhymes
of Emily Dickinson, aslant. I slide my Truths
across the room, daring anyone
to make me rhyme.

---

*Baka means stupid.

Saturday Matinee II ~ Pacific Hell

Six American hostages,
nurses with torn blouses
and dirt-smudged cheeks,
huddle in a grass shack,
Japanese prisoners of war.

This World War II drama
on a steamy Pacific island
is our adolescent notion
of a *fun* afternoon.

Buxom beauties
with determined faces
snarl like wolves.
I feel their fear cut through me
like a sword through silk.

The brunette snaps,
I'd rather kill myself
than let a Jap touch me.

Freddy grabs the popcorn,
the message is personal,
we know the drill,
jump for the exits.

We emerge in sunshine
as Japanese soldiers
on downtown Seattle
sidewalks marching in step,
endowed with a touch that makes
white women desire death.

My jungle spirits throttled —
I fear they will emerge,
extend hands deep in pockets.

I need a warning label,
a sign around my neck
to walk these streets,
touching me may be
hazardous to your health.

Saturday Matinee III ~ Mickey Rooney Does Yellow Face

As a child I worship Mitsu Arakawa,
Kenji Shibuya, and Tosh Togo —
Japanese professional wrestlers:
sly, sneaky, underhanded, and mean.
I aspire to kick and karate chop
blond Gorgeous George,
pummel him into four
levels of unconsciousness.

In 1960 Hollywood, Asians
were not qualified
to wrap a wet towel
around potbelly midriffs or
lean over a New York apartment
movie set dripping wet
to fracture English and holler
through a mouth full
of buck teeth, *Miss Gorightly*.

As a teenager, I dream
of Madison Square Garden,
where Marilyn Monroe
is sewn into a white dress,
waddles to the mike and sings
"Happy Birthday" to President Kennedy.

In that garden, wrestling crowds boo
my Japanese regalia.
I stomp and throw salt,
sumo ritual to purify the air.

Raise my right fist,
swagger like a villain.
Climb the corner turnbuckle.

I rejoice in the falseness of this vision,
more righteous than being a real
Mickey Rooney with buck teeth
in yellow face.

Oh, what I would give for a Japanese movie —
actors with small noses in whiteface
fracturing English.

Japanese Movie Night

Samurai-ghost movie night
at the Seattle Buddhist Church —
camera pans the forest pines,
focuses on a woman's back,
red kimono and flowing black hair.
She hums a sad melody.
Her lantern, a twisted branch
with flames on each end,
is gripped between her teeth.

In moonlight she pounds
a wooden peg into a pine tree,
the mallet head strikes and clacks
against her soft wailing.

Camera dollies in for a head shot.
Quickly she turns 180 degrees
and reveals a blank visage,
image that fills the screen.
The crowd screams and my mouth
drops as my mind won't accept
what I see and can't see.

A few nights later TV brings
Victory at Sea in the Pacific
with enemies who look like me.
Captured Japanese parade in dirty loin cloths,
prisoners with arms in the air
blasted from palm trees
and flamed out of caves.

In kindergarten, I mumble the flag salute.
Anxiously I await the day my classmates' eyes
turn toward Santa and the holidays.
On December 7, I cover my face
and lie low like a forest ghost
with my hands thrust among sword ferns.

Part IV:
Minidoka Aftermath

"When World War II started, they forced us to leave home and I didn't want to go. When the war ended they kicked us out of camp even though we had nowhere to go."

~ Hanae Matsuda

Vacation

When he hands
over the keys,
the resort owner
doesn't say "Jap."

Marlboro butts
afloat in half-empty
Rainier Beer bottles
in the cabin tell all.

Mother rolls her sleeves,
brushes sudsy ammonia across linoleum,
fruit flies feasting on wine dregs scatter.

Let's go home, we plead.

Mom ignores us,
dips her wrinkled hands,
scrubs brown stains
from the toilet bowl,
mops sandy corners,
and pulls silky webs from rafters.

Outside the cabin,
barefoot boys and girls frolic.
To them I am the gardener,
houseboy, janitor,
Charlie Chan's blithering son
holding a mop — but
never a blond girl's hand
in a game of Red Rover.

Like paper cutouts they stand.
I hop with excitement and grit my teeth,
Call me from shadows, I pray,
I can break the line.

Idaho Homesteader

Like gandy dancers pounding spikes
for the Great Northern Railroad,
German Americans straddle
our former Minidoka barrack,
cut a straight kerf through this
1948 land lottery prize.

Twin Falls church elders
in canvas overalls and heavy black shoes
gather for the house raising —
chop wood, fill cracks,
pound six penny nails
straight into barrack bones.

Tight grain lumber
traps Minidoka sorrow.
Letters from Italy and Hiroshima
once tacked here.
White paint covers all.

Does anything remain of us?
I wonder — *Did they find*
my matchstick darts,
marbles buried by the stairs,
or touch my dreams
crumpled like red and white
Babe Ruth wrappers
lodged in cracks?

Mom's Trunk

A pink baby dress,
gift from Quakers,
is folded lovingly
next to a red kimono sash
with embroidered golden crane.
Pressed like a leaf in a Bible,
the garment carried hope
of a future granddaughter.

As a kindergartner I remember
Mr. Bonus, a jolly white man
with rosy cheeks and a brown suit.

He is a joyous surprise.
I never know why he gives me
Jack 'n Jill and *Boys' Life*
magazine subscriptions.

I believe everyone has a Mr. Bonus,
someone real — not like
the Easter Bunny or the Tooth Fairy.
Mother says he is a friend,
even when his visits end.

Forty years later, when Mom is
in Maryland, she steals a side trip
to Quaker headquarters in Philadelphia,
leaves a handwritten *thank you* note
for the Minidoka layette, dress,
and postwar visits from Mr. Bonus.

I learn Bonus is just a man
delivering hope for the "Friends."
Would it surprise him to see me now
balancing a wine glass
of Merlot and gripping a plate
with yellow satay chicken skewers
and stuffed mushroom caps
at a black-tie fund-raiser?
I'd like to think not.

Wearing a silk bow tie and 14-karat gold
lapel pin, I am that child, sans blond hair,
blue shorts, and knee socks from *Boys Life,*
whistling as I march up mountain trails, child
who becomes a man never forgetting
the kindness of Santa dressed in brown.

Today I surprise Michele, Allison's
six-year-old daughter. I bring
a pink plush rabbit, *Max and Ruby* videos,
and "how to" books about leading
a fairy's life, kindness with a boomerang
meant for me.

Mary's High School Graduation

for Carole's mother

In a 1942 senior class photo,
Mary's Japanese American face nestles
between four white boys who sport
wire frame glasses and slick hair.

Her dog-eared graduation presentation
brims with hope and innocence,
speech practiced but never delivered
is stuck between pages
of her *Skagina* high school annual.
FBI curfew prevents her
from attending graduation.

She shuts her room door,
cradles her *Skagina*
like an old teddy bear.
To an imaginary audience
she tearfully recites her speech by heart.

Crossing the Tule Lake concentration camp gates,
Mary is unfinished, incomplete, and not blessed.
Skagina, a comforting reminder of better times —
best wishes from friends, sketches, cartoons,
and treasured memories.

Fifty years later, fate beckons Mary.
She packs the Nissan van,
boards the Bainbridge Island ferry
with her daughter and two grandchildren
for the sixty-mile drive to high school.

Pomp and Circumstance plays.
Aisles teem with bulldog cutouts,
green banners, and white streamers.

Mary nods as the crowd welcomes her
with a standing ovation and applause.
Strangers cheer for this small woman
who once walked these halls
as a student, friend, and classmate.

Like Lady Liberty
in a flowing green gown
and stiff mortar board,
she raises her head,
pulls the robe to the side, and
steps toward the stage.

She prays this ceremony will end
her slow-motion nightmares:
floundering and groping through
a merry-go-round high school maze
in search of a diploma.

Confetti tumbles like cherry blossoms,
248 green tassels turn.
Mortar boards fly like frightened birds,
graduates surround and embrace a tearful Mary,
steady her beyond the pop of camera flashes and cheers.

Skagina with 247 signatures and a message
is Mary's gift:

> *Never again will innocents be taken
> unjustly from this valley in silence.*
>
> *Class of 1992*

.

Legacy

When hecklers circle a north Seattle
mosque after 9-11,
I won't turn my back
in silence knowing vultures
will descend on shuttered stores
and homes when hate
stains holy walls.

Who will stand
on granite mosque stairs,
link arms with brown brothers
and sisters?

I will stand for my
mother and father,
who sixty years ago
could not against US Army
bayonets, Browning rifles,
President Roosevelt
and Executive Order 9066.

I am like an alien abductee
who walks among
the living knowing the pain
and humiliation of being taken
while most white
Americans look away.

I have no nightmares about
gray creatures with spindly fingers
pushing needles into my belly button.
My stomach is a chunk of black basalt,
heavy like a meteorite, weight
that disappears only when I stand.

With only one lifetime to swing a pick,
toss dirt, haul ore, I hoist a lantern
in black tunnels, slide my hands
to atomic bonds, meld them
with stalactites and stalagmites of justice.

Part V:
Friends & Family

Wisp of a Gal *for Tess*

Sun blazes on a September afternoon.
I perch cool in a pear tree
above zucchinis and cherry tomatoes,
study the world like a crouching ninja.

A vision appears:
aerodynamic fins, wraparound windshield
and jet aircraft grill on a '51 Buick Le Sabre
idling at a stoplight, hubcaps spin,
my eyes whirl — kaleidoscope colored chunks
slide and twist until images click into focus. I see

Tess styling in a faux fur coat
and Dr. Zhivago Russian winter hat
hiding a short bob. With perfect eyebrows,
thin and clean and eyeglasses dangling from a chain,
she chauffeurs me in Ray's gun-metal-gray Mercedes
through downtown Port Angeles,
former bustling hub of boat builders with leather aprons
and wool shirt lumberjacks,
town weathered and shopworn by salty winds that
rise off the Strait of Juan de Fuca.

Her Irish brogue rolls like tapioca pearls,
mellifluous melodies and rhythms
that remind me of cigars and a squeeze box
harmonica player who cradles Irish whiskey bottles,
stomps his boots on stage while rosy cheeked women
bust a lusty river dance jig on a warehouse floor.

I hear horses clopping as a wisp of a girl,
Tess, with long brown hair,
a young Lady Godiva in overalls, gallops
past the Deer Park drive-in theatre,
hive where she and her high school
sweetheart smooch behind steamy windows
like a stack of pancakes hot off the griddle.

Cinema's hour-glass queen of cleavage, lips, and kisses
incinerates the big screen: Marilyn Monroe wiggles,
raises one leg at the knee, flipping up her skirt
with a high heel kick, her gluteus is maximus,
like pears hostage under a tight red sheen,
twenty pounds of rice in a ten-pound bag.

I stretch for one more juicy treasure,
another sensual teardrop,
anticipate holding the pulsating oblong orb
of erotic and earthy fire overflowing
with so much ripeness that the tree
cannot hold it another instant.

Vertigo spins me upside down.
I am a teenage Icarus with aerodynamic fins,
wraparound windshield, embracing the wind like
a young girl fluttering with billowing brown hair
away, away on horseback.

Careening Toward Forever-After
for Tess

In reverse I stomp the gas pedal.
Aluminum bends and screeches like
a wounded brontosaurus.

My shrimp fishing checklist for 4:00 AM:
license, lunch, and *life preserver*.
Open the garage door, not on the list.

Twisted rollers off track
hang cattywampus.
Dislodged metal sections dangle
like a dismembered tin man dancing.
Dorothy and Toto would drop
their jaws in disbelief.

If my antiquated cell phone were capable,
I would tweet and text
about how to mangle a garage door,
or I'd post a photo on Facebook
with me flipping Luddite yellow pages
under a superimposed Eiffel Tower.

I muscle broken sections
like a Houdini weightlifter act.
Chevy exhaust pipe belches a cloud.
Metallic echoes still pinball my brain.
A crumpled door, wrecked accordion
gleams sunshine behind me.

On the water fishing, my world is transformed
into a modern El Greco's *Storm over Toledo* —
Space Needle and Seattle skyline
to the east and snow covered Olympics to the west.

Riding Elliot Bay whitecaps I ponder:
small prehistoric armored warriors
with prickly swords — shrimp as sushi, fried,
grilled, boiled, poached, and barbecued Bubba Gump style.

Tugging 400 feet of leaded line,
water trickles like icicles melting.
Arms burn, shoulders ache,
and I wonder, *When will this torture end?*
Color appears as the trap surfaces,

one hundred spot-tail shrimp hop,
twist, and bubble out of the cage
like effervescent champagne.
I snap shrimp heads, peel translucent armor,
and chomp crunchy tails.

When I was a child, Aunt Mitsumori bribed me
with a nickel to release
a spider from a Mason jar.

What would she say about panic cries
from shrimp destined for a dip into wasabi
and soy, drop-kicked into my Nirvana?

Did they bathe in a loving tunnel of white light
and meet a friendly face
or encounter infinite fields of emptiness?

Under the sign of two fish facing each other,
I pass myself resting in deep pools
and discover a Moon child, Tess,
Pacific Northwest Dungeness,
not a soft shell crustacean.

Careening toward forever-after
and Grand Canyons of outer space,
Tess, what do you think about
when you think about crashing
through garage doors?

Jan's Houseboat

Saint Knute party revelers huddle — bump elbow, to elbow,
rub back to back, and balance drinks and hors d'oeuvres
like contestants in a three-legged race, leaving stains
and red wine glass petrogylph rings in their wake.
Champagne sloshes from crystal glasses,
effervescence fizzles on white carpets.

Sturdy like a hobbit's cottage in the shire,
Jan's houseboat lists, struggles
under excess party weight.
Water seeps under the front door jamb.

I recall a Filipino ferry flips in roiling seas
as excited passengers dash to the rail
when airborne porpoises break water,
something like the fully clothed partygoer,
glass in hand, who flies
off Jan's porch into Lake Union
chasing imaginary dragonflies.

Jan steadies a boiling pot of *akvavit*,
cauldron of orange alcohol, caraway, and dill,
Vahalla gift from Odin for heroic warriors,
favored elixir of brave Knute, drink that
greases his slide into sainthood.

This is not a last dance on the Titanic
where the band plays to a sinking crowd.
Revelers gather food trays and alcohol,
export the party next door,
including the pot of boiling potatoes
and *lefse* pancakes. Legend has it
that mad Irishmen pelt raider ships with
a hurricane of potatoes, driving Norsemen
off course and out of their minds.

Calm returns as Paige performs her cello solo,
sad riffs in memory of Dave and Peg, her parents,
victims of Alaska Flight 261 from Puerto Vallarta.
Fleeting moments we share when Fratelli's
4th of July fireworks burst overhead.
Booms vibrate in our chests,
dead embers shower our heads. Navy choppers
hoist illuminated American flags in darkness
before the Lake Union sky ignites.
Copter blades churn and reverberate
to sounds of Wagner's *Flight of the Valkyries*,
homage to Coppola's *Apocalypse Now* —
where squadrons of Huey gunships emerge from smoke
in dragonfly formations strafing Viet Cong villages,
then dive like eagles straight into the heart of victory.

Fifteen Love, the E-mail Slam

I barely crack Tess's e-mail door,
her words and images thunder past
like Road Runner and Wile E. Coyote
zipping down a canyon.
I am taken by a whirlwind,
twist like a Saturday morning cartoon tornado,
search for a salmon net racket
to return what must be the fifteen-love ace shot,
on one knee I try a volleyball dig.

Slip-stream vapor trails appear,
vacuum me like a Hoover upright
going sixty on a tight-weave carpet,
rip tides push flotsam.
Moses parts the Red Sea,
chance to catch the dervish of kisses
while her red babushka flaps,
cruising top down on a zigzag street
after her slam.

I imagine me as a gangster in a double-breasted
suit with white wing-tip shoes,
I call her "Doll," this
horned-rimmed woman
who loves cokes and popcorn,
especially old maids
she cracks like Wrigley's gum.

Her fishnet stockings
packed with Howitzers
swivel as if on turrets,
recall the sepia photo of her
mother posing and stretching seductively
against a World War II Sherman tank.
Exhausted, we crumple and fall into
each other. We are a half-eaten bag,
butter stains upholstery and each other
as if we were sixteen forever.

Taste of Freedom

Mrs. Pepper, Quaker visitor,
shares treasures from
beyond the barbed wire.
Five-year-old Hisako
embraces her birthday present
of Spam, which hibernates on an icy sill.

Hisako pinches crumb-sized
nubs of brown between
her thumb and index finger.
Gleefully she nibbles a greasy morsel,
corrals a guilty grin.

She licks her fingers clean
and wraps wax paper over slices
and tucks Raggedy Ann in bed.
She cradles her salty pleasure —
an offering to her ancestors —
Daiji na mono, precious thing,
ambrosia for morning.

Years pass and Hisako
never opens another can of Spam,
embarrassed that she once
coveted compressed pink in a tin,
gelatinous glob that comedians call
Something Posing As Meat.

Back home I chat with Sue, an old friend,
in a Seattle breakfast joint.

She fingers her coffee mug and
mentions returning to Hawaii,
slips into a little pidgin,
*How you figga dis haole kine chow?**

Kitchen doors bursts open.
The cook is a Bluto look-alike
wearing a trapeze T-shirt
and hair net straight out of
a *Popeye* comic.

His ham-sized hands flap;
eagerly he invites us
into his kingdom.

>   *From Hawaii bro?* he asks.
>   *Special treat for bot of you.*
>   *Tastes just like home.*

He puffs his chest like
an award-winning French chief,
proudly unveiling a chunk
of glistening Spam flanked
by pineapple chunks.

We sit down and poke forks
into his notion of our delicacy.
I never reveal my Spam history
or not growing up in the Islands.
Who would have thought camp
flashbacks could appear glazed, so adorned
for our reunion?

**Rough translation — How do you figure (or what do you make of) this white person's
kind of idea of food?*

La Medusa Cooking Class*
for Chef Julie

If I am Semolina,
Jules scoops handfuls of me,
chops spinach, mixes parsley.
Egg yolks cement a green lump.

With loving thumps and tender spanks,
she wraps me tight in saran.
I burst when her red lips
caress my roundness. Wooden rolling pins
and wine bottles whirl.

With a crank of the pasta machine
she squeezes me flat,
presses me to her cheeks,
then drapes me over wooden dowels.
I am stretched — green-chalk-ugly,
flaccid and grainy.

Jules teases green bow ties,
curls angel hairs and fettuccine ribbons.
She spares napalm garlic
and dresses me with simmering duck legs,
aubergine figs, fresh peas, cracked olives,
topped with pea vines.

One mouthful of green
and she is my pasta slave.

---

*In honor of the June 7, 2009 cooking class conducted by Chef Julie Andres.
Menu: *Aqua pazzo soup, fresh noodles with peas and morel mushrooms, and zabaglione.*
Wines: *Stern Sauvignon Blanc, Domaine de Fontsainte "gris de Gris," and Malmsey Maderia.*

Woman Who Paints With Fire

for Etsuko Ichikawa

Pot of green tea steams
near a porcelain cup.

Seven-year-old Etsuko
slides Aida sensei's studio door.
The room is a hive, a bear's den,
magician's lair littered
with worn paintbrushes
and rice paper stacked
on dusty shelves.

Etsuko runs her fingers across
brown horsehair brushes.
Dust flies and sparkles in shafts
streaming through windows —
magical sparks, fireflies.

Small spirits shift,
their eyes follow her as she examines
the folding chair, worn table,
wooden floor, and paints.

*Otosan** hangs a western suit
he crafts from blue gabardine
milled in Kyoto.

Otosan, Etsuko asks, *where is Aida sensei?*
Her father smiles and says,
Sometimes artists become invisible.
He places his index finger to his lips,
points to a small sliding door,

where Aida sensei hides when
he wishes not to be disturbed.
Walking the cobblestones home, *otosan* asks,

What did you see?
Did you notice the shadows,
patterns on the floor,
steam rising from the teapot
and smell freshness flushing the musty air out?

At home in Tokyo,
Etsuko and her family
stand at the upstairs window,
stare into the sunset, draw pictures.
They laugh out loud —
Etsuko sketches a cat on a fence,
otosan the clouds and *okasan** tree shadows.

Etsuko begins her spirit journey
as a young woman.
She dreams of Aida sensei's
hiding place, her mind wanders
into the imaginary lair,
where sweet musk inhabits.

Fireflies drive her from hiding,
teach her secrets — how heat transforms,
how to wield a molten wand like a samurai.

Ten years later and five
thousand miles away,
her arms grow weary
twirling fiery orange globes
in a green Northwest rain forest.
Etsuko's body remembers
soul patterns *otosan* taught —
how light strikes the floor,
fabrics fall — bunch, drape,
and rise in glowing bursts.

Like a goddess she
whirls molten rivers in her orbit
and singes wave patterns into glass.
Her fire creations begin
with a prayer, meditation,
and a memory: of when
she stands with her family
at the window upstairs,
coaxing the sunset onto paper —
soaked with carmine and royal blue,
impulse to impulse, reds and yellows
to help a sunset linger on her page.

---

*Otosan is father and Okasan is mother.

Reunion Sara & Charlie

I grow dizzy in the 90 degree Arizona heat telling
Seattle stories about how the Trojans lost
their Rose Bowl bid in Saturday's horizontal rain.

The VW churns up the dirt driveway
off Buckeye Road past a date palm grove,
trailers, and windmill next to the one-bedroom adobe.
Dust blows into the Levis drying on the line.

Ace, B.J. and Susie — the dogs — bark their greetings.
Sara sits in a rocking chair on the front porch,
Charlie leans against the house smoking a pipe.
We each sip a Hamms and watch the sun set
over the Palo Verde Nuclear site.

> *It's good to see you, Sara grins.*
> *Lately my vision gets blurry*
> *and I have some paralysis*
> *in my right hand and leg.*
> *Tomorrow I'm going into Tempe*
> *for another EEG and CAT scan.*
> *We would have told you sooner but were*
> *afraid you wouldn't come.*

When the desert sky darkens,
Charlie drags out a lawn chair,
focuses his telescope
on the night sky. Sara gazes
at her star map and exclaims,

Sometimes we see satellites go by.

A shooting star, I holler and point too late.

Space trash, comes the reply.

> *A deep brain mass, not a tumor:*
> *space garbage in the brain,*
> Sara proclaims, *just like my X-rays.*
> *Can't complain though,*
> she smiles, *it's steak tonight at Tonopah Joe's*
> *with my two favorite men.*

May the Love*

Whoosh, Whoosh,
kill a king salmon
and call the priest.

Seems like yesterday
my wife does the *whoosh whoosh*,
Gregory can't stop smiling.
Didn't expect that from a redneck.

So Suzie it is time
for another black sambuca.
Rob offers a toast,
When the saints rise up
I want to be pampered like Gregory.
May the love in this heart pass through
these hands to you.

Gregory's psychedelic pig runs
snowy trails of the great Northwest.
Into the wilderness with chocolate
sticking to the roof of its mouth,
it squeals, *Made it through another*
Thanksgiving.

I discover I love fennel
and Sue's new kitchen,
reach another summit,
in nostalgia: say *My oh my*
laughter is lovely.

Group poem — each person contributes a line at Gregory's 59th birthday party.

In Memory of Kip

Tess, the day I received your last poem
from Ireland about your brother's illness,
my friend, Kip, died of a heart attack
casting trout lines on a small Whidbey Island lake.

Shocked and brain tired,
I consult your imagination
where Native American visions reside.

You instruct me to build a driftwood bonfire at midnight
on Alki beach, near the stone lighthouse on the Salish Sea,
where silver salmon school in green kelp beds.
Orange flames explode gnarled limbs and branches
as they spark into crackling fireflies.
Smoke sprints north over the bay
like skywriting vapor trails, leaving charcoal
for war paint and petroglyph drawings.

You share a prayer with me,
Nam-Myoho-Renge-Kyo,
mystical Buddhist sutra of the Lotus
unfolding to enlightenment.

I strike the brass singing bowl.
Clear like a cast-iron bell it rings. Then
crisp high pitch fades to a thin thread.
Echoes call bald eagles nesting
in cedars above the sandy cliffs.
Under a full moon,
above roiling whitecaps,
black-and-white messengers glide,
dive and summon the Orca pods.

A fisherman king has died.

Part VI:
The Way Infinity Turns

Ukulele Band *for AC Arai & the Kimochi Band*

Japanese women single file
on the Minidoka reunion stage
strum rhythms that twist
like the road to Hana, Hawaii.

Aloha muumuus sway,
pink and turquoise designs flutter,
ukulele music spirals back
on itself like infinity.

I smell plumeria and feel
the warm trades blowing,
remember picking
red mountain apples
halfway up the road to Hana.
Hour-glass-shaped apples,
crunch-crisp
and sweet to the core.

Fresh opihi, limpets,
like miniature abalone
under Chinese hats
layered in kelp,
stacked in a metal pan
at the Hana General Store.
Metallic rainbow shells glisten.

Ukuleles strum rhythms
like infinity turning.
A third grader describes

it as *uni-singing*,
music that makes him hum.

All are welcome to the band,
some battle cancer as they sway.
A dozen gray haired women,
different but the same.

One looks like Mom
dancing in a muumuu
before lymphoma takes her.
Molecular structures
entwine with the music.

I dream of strumming
away all my Minidokas
and touching sadness
everyone carries
who lived there.

My songs bend back
on themselves,
the way infinity turns.
With each stanza and line,
I yearn for the last Minidoka echo,
veil where sorrow ends
and the road to Hana's
white concrete horse and buggy
bridges, turquoise lagoons,
cascading waterfalls,
and Seven Sacred Pools begin.

Mother Passes

Her wandering spirit returns
to Block 26 barrack two,
our wartime home,
now a cozy German American
homesteader's house.

She settles like dust
on a patchwork quilt.
Somewhere there is a birdhouse
nailed to the barrack.
Paint and floral wallpaper
cover bare wood,
a silver teapot whistles
on the iron potbelly stove.

Blue-eyed baby with rosy cheeks
mouths a plastic rattle,
lurches and giggles happily.
Young blond woman,
long hair tied in a bun,
unbuttons her gingham dress,
bares her full pink breast.

Mom smiles and steps into the light,
grasps *jichan's** hand,
glows incandescent with joy
knowing she nurtured me
beyond Minidoka's shadows
and barbed wire.

Home alone that night,
I hear a chair drag across
the dining room floor.

* *Grandfather in Japanese.*

Salmon Dreams I ~ The Priest

King salmon breaks water,
shakes, rips line. Silver flashes race
through Point Defiance green waters
until a speckled tail slaps the deck.
I grab the "priest," bloodstained deliverer,
gnarly knot of absolution.

At the office I am a lump in a cubicle
framed by pea-green institutional walls
under a fluorescent glow.
My eyes cross and weave e-mail strings.
On the water life and death
are in my hands — with a thump
scales fly helter-skelter.

I strip orange egg skeins,
cradle them on ice.
Slice red flesh from bones
and toss innards to gulls.

I savor and taste the fight again.
Primordial energies
transport me to the first
native who pulls
a salmon to shore.

I am a boxer after twelve rounds,
imagine crowds standing and cheering
as I ride their shoulders.
Adrenaline pumps victory
gushing through my veins
like a rush of shaking wildness
until exhaustion overcomes
and arrogance ebbs.

Is gratitude enough
for taking a life?
Why do I believe salmon
desire death by my hands?
Pride is the sin of angels
and fishermen.

Salmon Dreams II ~ The Haunting

Without brakes squealing
or horns honking, a humpback
smashes our stern. We swirl,
and tip side to side —
flee the cabin like drunks
from a long night's ravage.

Clutching the "priest,"* I rip open
a life vest and flail
like a cartoon rag doll
tossed rail to rail.

Rising from the chaos,
Ahab's spirit beckons
from a nimbus of snarled ropes,
tangled harpoons.
Deliver me home, he calls,
I am ashes in the sea.

Horizon disappears
as we dive into the trough,
reappear at the crest.
Salt water spray cascades,
the "priest" tumbles,
from the ice chest into the mist.

Captain Lou cracks the cabin door,
scans the deck to see if
I am a popsicle bobbing in whitecaps.
Up north an Eskimo villager
fell through ice last year, certain
death for most. I wonder
what he thinks to keep
from freezing as hours pass until
his rescue.

One summer I jump into
the Tokeen, Alaska, bay.
Icy waters take my breath,
cold so intense my ancestors scream.

I imagine Japanese adventurers
shuffling straw slippers over snowy trails
crossing the land bridge thousands of years ago.

Unfortunates starve and freeze
on Alaskan glaciers, like the Donner Party
traveling the Oregon Trail, same path
Japanese concentration camp prisoners
ride in 1942, past memorials
where early emigrants die.
Near the Craters of the Moon, Japanese
in reverse migration push
on to Minidoka without mules,
oxen, great white whale, Ahab,
or gnarly priest to grant absolution.

They had each other. Men and women
with strong backs who raised children
and transformed desert
into sugar beet and potato fields.

They had each other until barracks are shuttered,
electricity disconnected, windows boarded
one by one and Minidoka is plowed under
as a misbegotten footnote in American history.

My fifth grade spirits rose and crashed
when the national *Weekly Reader*
newspaper features the camps.
America, it reports, *rationed necessities like
butter, gasoline, and meat during war —
internment was the Japanese
American patriotic sacrifice.*

---

*Nickname for the club or bonker to hit the fish on the head.

Salmon Dreams III ~ Salmon Rise

Under an Alaskan full moon,
thousands of silver mantles flash,
armored predators
navigate by stars, taste
streambeds of home,
fresh ribbons trickling
into the Pacific.

Those that slip hooks
live to twist in shallows.
Instinct electrifies
withering muscles,
defends encapsulated progeny.

Gravel boils and sprays.
Symphonic melodies,
photographic negative, an impression
etched in limbic memories
evoke a once-in-a-lifetime dance.

What guides my path —
Minidoka past,
free will, or fate?
I fight upstream, hand to hand,
or should I wait on the beach?

Words and images are my arrows,
ability to change my shield.
Under the sign of two fish
facing opposite directions,
I walk the road home alone.
And it is sweet to say "home"
even as I swim past myself
resting in swirling deep pools.

Faceless

*After the 9.0 earthquake, Japan pushes
eight feet closer to America,
shortens the day by 1.6 microseconds.*

Sendai is a garbage dump cut by a straight-shot road.
Pervasive stench of fish rotting
amid rubble. Another odor tinged
with a peculiar ripe edge swirls.
CNN body-blind cameras never show
arms, feet, chins protruding from heaps.

Behind thin flashlight beams, clothed in jump suits,
the faceless 50 march into their radioactive tombs.
What are they thinking as they slog
toward molecular disruption, staggering
this slow road to hell, these men
who look like me?

In the local high school gym
old Japanese men and women
who could be my *bachan**and *jichan,**
ashamed of their torn straw slippers,
silently line up for water,
a bowl of hot ramen. How to bear
the unbearable with dignity,
their karmic message.

I pour a guilty cup of creamed coffee
and escape the CNN periscope-eye
of suffering with the flick of a switch.

Images of atomic Hiroshima linger:
my grandfather's home, where a road cuts
past his obliterated life through stacks
of charred and twisted bodies. An eighty-year-old man
pushes a wooden cart. With each step in this wasteland
his red slippers flap.

I vow to return to Fukushima,
walk places my friends cherished back in 1995,
kneel and pray for those missing forever,
strike the temple bell.
Near the Fuji apple orchard
and house I stayed in years ago,
I will recall the faceless 50,
then pinch incense between
thumb and index finger,
raise the fragrance to my forehead and release powder
into a smoldering bowl of ashes.
For an instant,
I am no longer *gaijin*,
foreigner.
I am Japanese.
Watashi wa Nihonjin desu.

Back in Hiroshima,
my hands sink deep
into what was
radioactive soil.
I become another
faceless foreigner
who mourns in a land
he can never call home.

*Bachan is grandmother
and Jichan is grandfather.

San Francisco J-Town

CNN warns Sendai radioactivity
will pass over San Francisco tonight,
Trace amounts
could fall with rain —
less than an airplane trip,
tooth X-ray, a fraction
of what a banana emits.
I pop open my tourist umbrella,
search for a steaming bowl of
pork ramen,
grin like a butterscotch cowboy riding a
chocolate stallion clopping
down Post Street near Japantown. My heels
snap pavement like a flamenco dancer.

I recall Chilean miners
chant soccer cheers
buried 250 feet deep in darkness,
rise one by one to the sunshine
like torpedoes. There is no uplifting rescue
for Sendai.
Eighty-year-old Japanese farmers
with white bandanas
light cigarettes,
mop slimy toxins,
sacrifice their health
so young Japanese cowboys and cowgirls
can stomp, can punish muddy puddles.

Tsunami Letter ~ March 2011

Shunning the safety of high ground
when the tide rips and sirens howl,
I will head out to sea as in Hokusai's painting.

Only now do we understand
the ferocious curl of those painted waves.
Before the first deadly one crashes
abolishing shores, I touch Japanese collective
memories of waves past, locked
in my American bones.

I am brimming with wave fractals,
variations of the same pattern
repeating over centuries, folktales
of Momotaro, the boy hero spawned
from a giant peach to slay demons and ogres,
and the Shimomura brothers, samurai who commit
double suicide — stabbing and slashing each other,
face to face until they are waves, simply
crashing across each other's shoulders.

When my bones wash ashore,
burn them in a stack of driftwood.
Open them with flames and smoke their
cacophony of ashes in sky-swirl,
spread them across miles
of beach and cloud drift.
Memories like a million
radioactive particles escape,
glow, and flutter toward

the lights of San Francisco,
the wheat fields of Kansas,
then fall like a rain
of Japanese Icaruses
over America's heartland,
fragments of a forever foreigner
who insists on coming home.

Notes

1. The cover art, entitled **Forever Foreigner**, is from Shimomura's existing collection. Shimomura is in the center holding an umbrella. Matsuda wears Kabuki makeup and can be identified by his Minidoka concentration camp number, 11464D.

2. References to the psychiatrist Barry appear in the poem **Too Young to Remember** in Matsuda's book of poetry, A Cold Wind from Idaho.

3. For the **1943 Minidoka Camp Album**, the photograph referenced in the poem can be found in the Cabinet Makers group photo in the Engineering Section of the 1943 Minidoka Interlude camp album.

4. For **WWII Route to Freedom**, the illustration's title is **Night Watch**, which is from Shimomura's existing work.

5. For **They Turn Their Eyes Away**, anti-Japanese sentiment and prejudice persisted after the war. Anti-Japanese resettlement petitions were signed in some communities on the west coast. Grocery stores in Hood River, Oregon refused to sell food to returning Japanese.

6. For the **Idaho Concentration Camp Veil**, some women protected their modesty in the gang latrines by covering their faces. Some daughters held cardboard screens to shield their mothers in the latrine.

7. For **No No Darkness**, young Japanese American men who checked "No No" on two loyalty questions were called "No No Boys." Many of them were sent to federal prisons like the McNeil Island Penitentiary in Washington State. In 1957 John Okada's first novel, No No Boy, was published and dealt with the experiences of a "No No" boy in Seattle after the war. Jimi Mirikitani, subject of the movie Cats of Mirikitani, renounced his US citizenship during World War II and became homeless after the war.

8. For **Hiroshima Bomb**, Matsuda's relatives were in the family home one thousand meters from ground zero at the time of the bombing. Three Hiroshima poems about his relatives are contained in Matsuda's book of poetry, A Cold Wind from Idaho.

9. For **Gates of Dachau**, the US Army credits the 552nd Field Artillery Battalion of the all Japanese American 442nd Regimental Combat Team for the May 2, 1945 liberation of Kaufering IV, one of the sub-camps of Dachau.

10. **Saturday Matinee III ~ Mickey Rooney Does Yellow Face** refers to the 1961 movie *Breakfast at Tiffany's*, starring Audrey Hepburn and George Peppard. The movie was based on the novella of the same name by Truman Capote. Many famous movie stars and personalities donned "yellow face" in film and portrayed Asians. Marlon Brando, Sean Connery, Shirley Maclaine, Peter Lorre, Jennifer Garner, Sidney Toler and Warner Oland (two of the nine actors who played Charlie Chan), Ingrid Bergman, John Wayne, Peter Sellers, Katherine Hepburn, Fred Astaire, Mryna Loy, Ricardo Montalban, David Carradine, and Helen Hayes were among many who played Asians. Most of the list was found on: http://brightlightsfilm.com/18/18_yellow.php#.U08ZOOZdVZE.

11. For **Vacation**, the poem was inspired by Roger Shimomura's first vacation after the war when his family stayed at a Cannon Beach, Oregon, rental cabin. The painting is from Roger's existing collection.

12. For **Japanese Movie Night**, the Seattle Japanese Buddhist Church showed a Japanese movie double feature regularly for years after the war. Because no admission fee was charged after the second feature began, it became a gathering place for Japanese American teens who attended for free.

13. For the **Idaho Homesteader**, the US government conducted a land lottery for parcels of the closed Minidoka concentration camp. Each homestead winner was awarded two and one-half barracks in addition to the land. Only returning veterans were eligible to participate. After the land lottery was completed, no Japanese American veterans were awarded a homestead plot. Some of the barracks were remodeled and converted into homes or storage sheds and are still standing today.

14. The **Idaho Homesteader** painting is titled **The Game**, which is from Shimomura's existing collection.

15. For **Mary's High School Graduation**, local high schools, the University of Washington, and Seattle University conducted special graduation ceremonies in honor of Japanese American students who were not able to participate during World War II because of the forced incarceration.

16. **Wisp of a Gal, Careening Toward Forever After,** and **Fifteen Love, The E-mail Slam** are poems written by Matsuda in an exchange with Tess Gallagher, internationally known poet and widow of the writer Raymond Carver. The full collaboration, entitled *Pow! Pow! Shalazam!*, can be found at: http://plumepoetry.com/tag/lawrence-matsuda.

17. For **Mother Passes**, the poem references the fact that homesteaders remodeled the barracks and used them as homes. Often times the homesteaders used the potbelly stoves from the barracks for heat.

18. For the **Taste of Freedom**, Spam was one of several highly processed meat items available during World War II. Hawaiian soldiers from the 100th Division who fought with the 442nd Regimental Combat Team acquired a taste for Spam and made it a popular food item in Hawaii after the war. One popular dish created by Hawaiians was Spam *musubi*, which consisted of a slice of Spam on top of rice, wrapped in seaweed.

19. For **Woman Who Paints with Fire**, Estuko Ichikawa can be seen demonstrating her molten glass painting techniques on the web at: http://vimeo.com/27252835.

20. For the **San Francisco J-Town** illustration, radioactivity symbols are depicted drifting over the skyline.

21. For **Tsunami Letter March 2011**, the US government assigned each family/individual in the camps an identification number. The Matsuda family number was 11464. Lawrence's number was 11464D, his father was 11464A, mother 11464B, and brother 11464C.

Credits:

The author and artist wish to acknowledge G. Page Tanagi for his graphic art and layout skills; Dr. Roger Daniels, Charles Phelps Taft Professor Emeritus of History, University of Cincinnati, for his scholarly assistance; John Pierce for his proofreading expertise and advice; and Tess Gallagher for her years of inspiration and encouragement.

Cover artwork, *Forever Foreigner*, courtesy of Frank & Helen Wewers, Kansas City, MO.

Author:
Lawrence Matsuda

Lawrence Matsuda was born in Minidoka, Idaho Relocation Center during World War II. He and his family were among the approximately 120,000 Japanese Americans and Japanese held without due process for approximately three years or more. Matsuda has a PhD in education from the University of Washington and was a secondary teacher, university counselor, state level administrator, school principal, assistant superintendent, educational consultant, and visiting professor at Seattle University (SU).

In 2005, he and two SU colleagues coedited the book *Community & Difference: Teaching, Pluralism & Social Justice*, (Peter Lang Publishing, New York). It won the 2006 National Association of Multicultural Education Phillip Chinn Book Award. In July of 2010, his book of poetry, *A Cold Wind from Idaho*, was published by Black Lawrence Press in New York. His poems appear in *Ambush Review, Raven Chronicles, New Orleans Review, Floating Bridge Review*, Black Lawrence Press website, Poets Against the War website, *Cerise Press, Nostalgia Magazine, Plumepoetry, Malpais Review, Zero Ducats, Surviving Minidoka* (book), *Meet Me at Higo's* (book), *Minidoka - An American Concentration Camp* (book and photographs), *Tidepools Magazine*, and the *Seattle Journal for Social Justice*.

In addition, eight of his poems were interpreted in a sixty-minute dance presentation titled *Minidoka*, performed by Whitman College students in Walla Walla, Washington (2011).

Artist:
Roger Shimomura

Roger Shimomura's paintings, prints, and theater pieces address sociopolitical issues of ethnicity. He was born in Seattle, Washington, graduated from Garfield High School, but spent two early years of his childhood in Minidoka (Idaho), one of ten concentration camps for Japanese Americans during World War II.

Shimomura received a BA degree from the University of Washington, Seattle, and a MFA from Syracuse University in New York. He has had over 130 solo exhibitions of paintings and prints, and has also presented his experimental theater pieces at venues such as the Franklin Furnace, New York City; Walker Art Center, Minneapolis; and the Smithsonian Institution, Washington, DC. He is the recipient of more than thirty grants, of which four are from the National Endowment for the Arts. Shimomura has been a visiting artist and has lectured on his work at more than two hundred universities, art schools, and museums across the country.

Shimomura began teaching at the University of Kansas, Lawrence, in 1969. During his teaching career there, he was the first faculty member ever to be designated a University Distinguished Professor (1994), and receive the Higuchi Research Prize (1998) and the Chancellor's Club Career Teaching Award (2002). In 2004 he retired from teaching and started the Shimomura Faculty Research Support Fund to foster faculty research in the Department of Art.

Shimomura's work is in the permanent collections of more than one hundred museums nationwide. He is represented by Flomenhaft Gallery, New York City, and Greg Kucera Gallery, Seattle.

Also Available from

Lawrence Matsuda

A Cold Wind from Idaho

Published by Black Lawrence Press, New York ©2010

On February 19, 1942, President Franklin D. Roosevelt signed Executive Order 9066 resulting in a cataclysmic series of events affecting all persons of Japanese ancestry residing on the West Coast of the United States. Those Americans familiar with the Pacific Northwest Japanese American World War II experience will understand Matsuda's poetic imagery wrought by the title. The metaphor of freezing winter winds chilling the body and then entering the soul of those affected conveys fittingly how they braved, and survived the cold iciness of Idaho's winters while huddled in a primitive American barbed wire concentration camp.

— *Tetsuden (Tets) Kashima, University of Washington*